ideals®
CHRISTMAS

IDEALS PUBLICATIONS
NASHVILLE, TENNESSEE

ISBN 0-8249-5889-6
Published by Ideals Publications
A division of Guideposts
535 Metroplex Drive, Suite 250
Nashville, Tennessee 37211
www.idealsbooks.com

Printed and bound in Mexico by RR Donnelley

Editor, Marjorie L. Lloyd
Designer, Marisa Calvin

Cover image copyright © Linda Nelson. All rights reserved.

10 9 8 7 6 5 4 3 2 1

ACKNOWLEDGMENTS

CROWELL, GRACE NOLL. "Beneath the Winter Stars" from *Facing the Stars*. Copyright ©
1941 by Harper & Brothers; renewed © 1968 by Grace Noll Crowell. Used by permission
of HarperCollins Publishers. GUEST, EDGAR A. "Sleigh Bells" from *All In a Lifetime* by
Edgar A. Guest. Published by Reilly & Lee Co., 1938. Used by permission of M. Henry
Sobell, III. TABER, GLADYS. "The New Year" from *Stillmeadow Calendar*. Copyright ©
1967 by Gladys Taber. Published by J. B. Lippincott. Used by permission of Brandt &
Hochman Literary Agents, Inc. We sincerely thank those those authors, or their heirs, who
submitted original poems or articles to *Ideals* for publication. Every possible effort has been
made to acknowledge ownership of material used.

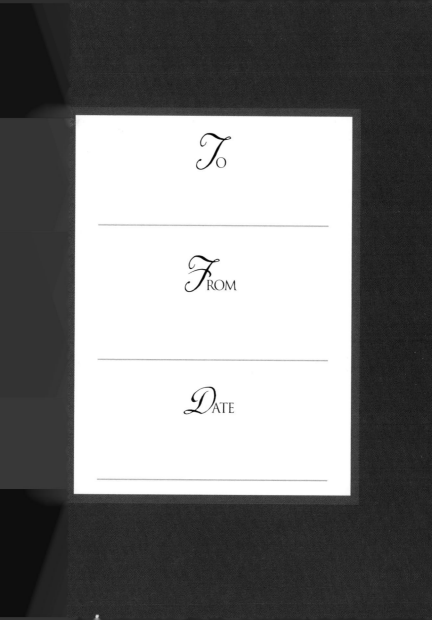

$\mathcal{T}$o

$\mathcal{F}$ROM

$\mathcal{D}$ATE

The Snowstorm

Ralph Waldo Emerson

Announced by all the trumpets of the sky,
Arrives the snow, and, driving o'er the fields,
Seems nowhere to alight: the whited air
Hides hills and woods, the river, and the heaven,
And veils the farmhouse at the garden's end.
The sled and traveler stopped, the courier's feet
Delayed, all friends shut out, the housemates sit
Around the radiant fireplace, enclosed
In a tumultuous privacy of storm.

    Come see the north wind's masonry.
Out of an unseen quarry evermore
Furnished with tile, the fierce artificer

Curves his white bastions with projected roof
Round every windward stake, or tree, or door.
Speeding, the myriad-handed, his wild work
So fanciful, so savage, naught cares he
For number or proportion. Mockingly,
On coop or kennel he hangs Parian wreaths;
A swan-like form invests the hidden thorn,
Fills up the farmer's lane from wall to wall,
Maugre the farmer's sighs; and, at the gate,
A tapering turret overtops the work.
And when his hours are numbered, and the world
Is all his own, retiring, as he were not,
Leaves, when the sun appears, astonished Art
To mimic in slow structures, stone by stone,
Built in an age, the mad wind's night-work,
The frolic architecture of the snow.

*E*VERY FERN IS
TUCKED AND SET,
'NEATH COVERLET,
DOWNY AND SOFT
AND WARM.
—SUSAN COOLIDGE

Photograph by Steve Terrill

Red Birds

Johnielu Barber Bradford

Four red birds hide
From sifting snow
Near my front door
Where cedars grow.
Four scarlet flames
Defy my gloom,
For soon I see
My cedars bloom!
No lovelier sight,
When red birds hide,
Except those specks
Close by their side—
Four dull, drab bits
Of snuggling down
Against red coats,
Four mates in brown.

Gift of the Starlings

Wanda A. Lyday

When the warm winds of summer awaken
Each elm tree and bright maple bough,
And the white rains at noontime have shaken
Green leaves where I wander now,
Then I shall remember the starlings
That came, with no glory of song,
To cherish beneath the roofs of their wings
The earth, here where I belong.
They did what they could when the sunless
Cold lay heavy and all was bare;
Their wings fell as softly as hands that bless
Or the sound of a silver tear.
Neither green leaves, nor gold sun shall hold me,
Nor lovelier wings that have flown;
I know every leaf will descend from the tree
And the starlings again claim their own.

Photograph by Steve Terrill

The Christmas Rose
Loise Pinkerton Fritz

When all the fields are winter lined
And brooks are frozen over,
When snowflakes trim the lofty pines
And days move forward slower,
When all the earth's December strewn,
The Christmas rose is then in bloom.

Winter Patterns
Mildred L. Jarrell

It's early morn and round about
Jack Frost has been so early out
Painting all the windows bright,
Tinting with his brush of white.
A gnarled old tree is bending down,
Rigid in her icy gown.
Meadowland's a frosty glow;
Earth lies sleeping 'neath the snow;
Crystal laces trim the hedge;
Scallops rim the window ledge;
Fairy patterns grace the door;
Wintertime is here once more.

Christmas waves a
magic wand over this world,
and, behold, everything is
softer and more beautiful.
—Norman Vincent Peale

Photograph by Carr Clifton

Snow Painting

Mary C. Ferris

The canvas is ready, the slope gleaming white,
Freshly covered with snowfall the previous night.
And now for the colors, the greens and the reds,
The bright little snowsuits of children with sleds.
In cap and mitt brilliant as wool can be dyed,
They weave in and out and they tumble and slide
Framed by my window, a picture that cheers
The grave and sedate hearts of our grown-up years.

The Presence of Snow

Eileen Spinelli

In the presence of snow,
weeds
become flowers,
fields
become
laughing feather beds.
In the presence of snow,
overcoats
fall to wings,
strangers
become angels.
Peace
becomes a familiar song,
in the presence of snow.

Sleighing Song

John Shaw

When calm is the night and the stars shine bright,
The sleigh glides smooth and cheerily;
And mirth and jest abound,
While all is still around,
Save the horses' trampling sound
And the horse-bells tinkling merrily.

Photograph by Nancy Matthews

SLEIGH BELLS

Edgar A. Guest

In forty years we've changed the world
And traded many things.
We've banished glowing stoves to gain
The warmth a furnace brings.
We've polished off discomforts with
Invention's magic art;
We've built the "press-the-button" age
When countless motors start.
But thinking of my boyhood days,
We lost a joy, I'll say,
When faithful horse and cutter were
Forever put away.
For when there comes a fall of snow,
I find for them I mourn
And that strap of tinkling sleigh bells
Supplanted with a horn.

We give up youth for mellow age;
Each forward step we take
To reach a joy which lies ahead
An old charm we forsake.
We deal and barter through the years
Old customs for the new,
Find easier ways to do the tasks
Once difficult to do.
But sometimes as we move along
To build the better day,
We learn we've been compelled to throw
A lovely thing away.
And thinking of my boyhood days
To this I will be sworn:
Sleigh bells sang a prettier song
Than any motor horn.

Hitch Old Dobbin to the Sleigh

Mamie Ozburn Odum

Hitch Old Dobbin to the sleigh;
We're going home today,
To holidays of long ago
Once more to romp and play.

There'll be fires of blazing logs,
Candlelight, and drifting snow,
With Grandpa and our Grandma
To grace the old wood door.

Oh, what a joyous greeting,
Halls trimmed in gold and green,
Tall trees with lights and glitter
Of every hue and sheen.

We're going home for Christmas
Where the cakes are spicy sweet,
With nuts and pies and candies
And a turkey stuffed to eat.

Hitch Old Dobbin to the sleigh;
Feel frosty winds of morn.
Listen! Hear the church bells ring,
Proclaiming Christ was born.

Christmastime, we're going home,
Sleighbells ringing all the way;
We'll sing songs as we glide along
This merry Christmas Day.

Photograph by William H. Johnson
Inset photograph by William H. Johnson

Christmas Greeting

Author Unknown

Sing hey! Sing hey!
For Christmas Day;
Twine mistletoe and holly,
For friendship glows
In winter snows,
And so let's all be jolly.

A Catch by the Hearth

Author Unknown

Sing we all merrily;
Christmas is here,
The day that we love best
Of days in the year.

Bring forth the holly,
The box, and the bay;
Deck out our cottage
For glad Christmas Day.

Sing we all merrily;
Draw around the fire,
Sister and brother,
Grandsire and sire.

Photograph by Larry LeFever/Grant Heilman

Homeward

Alice Kennelly Roberts

Our day's long search had ended
As evening shadows fell
And brought a triumph to the heart
Which words could never tell;
For though the cold nipped sharply
At fingers, ears, and toes,
We had our tree for Christmas
And now sought night's repose.

The last mile was the longest,
So very tired were we.
Dad pulled the sled; I held the tree,
And, then, home we could see.
Across the snow-swept distance
Our sleepy village lay,
With warmth of friends and loved ones
And happy Christmas Day.

How like our life's long journey,
The trail which Time has made.
The loved ones waiting for us,
The scenes which never fade,
The strength of Someone near us
To lift the heavy load—
These are memories we keep
To cherish on life's road.

THE SUPREME WORTH OF
TO LIFE, LIBERTY AND THE PU

Silhouette
June Masters Bacher

A silhouette of Christmastime
Reflects upon the snow,
Crisscrossing shadows merrily
As shoppers come and go.
They skate across the silver sheen
Made by the fragile ice,
Dart in and out of evergreen
That fills the air with spice.
They meet and greet on every street;
Then silently they part,
Bulging with packages that show
Each shadow has a heart.

It's beginning to look a lot like Christmas. . . .

Photograph by Henryk T. Kaiser/Grant Heilman

Christmas Angel

Virginia Blanck Moore

Half of me wants to throw away
This angel with damaged wings,
Stored in the attic at Yuletide's end
With leftover Christmas things.

Half of me sees that the gold
    on her robe
Is tarnished beyond repair,
And obviously the sheen is gone
From her halo-crowned, golden hair.

But half of me treasures the memories
That crowd as I hold her near,
Memories of all the joys she has seen
From her treetop year after year.

So I climb the ladder and put
    her there
In what is her rightful place,
Forgetting the injuries the years
    have brought—
She still has her angel face.

Though the glow she once had
Through the years may depart,
She retains, as always,
Her hold on the heart.

Photograph by Jessie Walker

Around the Hearth

Mildred L. Jarrell

It's still the same old fireplace,
Yet it has a special glow;
A great Yule log is burning
That we dusted clean of snow.

And spread above the mantel,
Scents of holly sprigs and spruce
Are mingling with the woodsmoke
Beneath our dear old roof.

This winter night the firelight
Fills us with a sense of peace,
And we share the rich blessings
Of a love that does not cease.

Now on the eve of Christmas,
With carolers singing near,
The hearth fire gives to all within
Its gifts of warmth and cheer.

Christmas Eve

Gail Brook Burket

We light a log fire on the hearth
And gather round its cheer
To sing the carols long beloved
When Christmastime is here.
And at our window we have set
A gleaming candle light,
Whose golden beams will shine afar
To welcome Him tonight.

Photograph by Jessie Walker

BITS & PIECES

Then sing to the holly, the Christmas holly,
That hangs over peasant and king.
—*Eliza Cook*

Perhaps the best Yuletide
decoration is being
wreathed in smiles.
—*Author Unknown*

Christmas may be a day of
feasting, or of prayer, but always
it will be a day of remembrance—
a day in which we think of
everything we have ever loved.
—*Augusta E. Rundel*

Oh! Holly branch and mistletoe.
And Christmas chimes wherever we go.
And stockings pinned up in a row!
These are thy gifts, December!
—*Harriet R. Blodgett*

The Christmas fires brightly gleam
And dance among the holly boughs.
—*Anne P. L. Field*

Christmas is the
season for kindling
the fire of hospitality
in the hall, the genial
flame of charity in
the heart.
　　　—*Washington Irving*

The holly and ivy about the walls wind
And show that we ought to our neighbors be kind.
　　　　　—*Author Unknown*

So, now is come our joyfullest feast,
Let every man be jolly;
Each room with ivy leaves is drest,
And every post with holly.
　　　—*George Wither*

The best of all gifts around any
Christmas tree: the presence of
a happy family all wrapped
up in each other.
　　　—*Burton Hillis*

The End of the Play

William Makepeace Thackeray

The play is done; the curtain drops,
    Slow falling to the prompter's bell:
A moment yet the actor stops,
    And looks around, to say farewell.
It is an irksome word and task;
    And, when he's laughed and said
        his say,
He shows, as he removes the mask,
    A face that's anything but gay.

One word, ere yet the evening ends,
    Let's close it with a parting rhyme,
And pledge a hand to all young friends,
    As fits the merry Christmastime.
On life's wide scene you, too, have parts
    That Fate ere long shall bid you play;
Good night! with honest gentle hearts
    A kindly greeting go always. . . .

Come wealth or want, come good or ill,
    Let young and old accept their part,
And bow before the Awful Will,
    And bear it with an honest heart,
Who misses or who wins the prize.
    Go, lose or conquer as you can;
But if you fail, or if you rise,
    Be each, pray God, a gentleman.

A gentleman, or old or young!
    (Bear kindly with my humble lays);
The sacred chorus first was sung
    Upon the first of Christmas Days:
The shepherds heard it overhead—
    The joyful angels raised it then:
Glory to Heaven on high, it said,
    And peace on earth to gentle men.

My song, save this, is little worth;
    I lay the weary pen aside
And wish you health, and love,
        and mirth,
    As fits the solemn Christmastide.
As fits the holy Christmas birth,
    Be this, good friends, our carol still—
Be peace on earth, be peace on earth,
    To men of gentle will.

*Photograph by Michael W.
Thomas/Grant Heilman*

A Merry Christmas from LITTLE WOMEN

Louisa May Alcott

Jo was the first to wake in the gray dawn of Christmas morning. No stockings hung at the fireplace, and for a moment she felt as much disappointed as she did long ago, when her little sock fell down because it was crammed so full of goodies. Then she remembered her mother's promise and, slipping her hand under her pillow, drew out a little crimson-covered book. She knew it very well, for it was that beautiful old story of the best life ever lived, and Jo felt that it was a true guidebook for any pilgrim going on a long journey.

She woke Meg with a "Merry Christmas" and bade her see what was under her pillow. A green-covered book appeared, with the same picture inside, and a few words written by their mother, which made their one present very precious in their eyes. Presently Beth and Amy woke to rummage and find their little books also, one dove-colored, the other blue, and all sat looking at and talking about them, while the east grew rosy with the coming day.

In spite of her small vanities, Margaret had a sweet and pious nature, which unconsciously influenced her sisters, especially Jo, who loved her very tenderly and obeyed her because her advice was so gently given.

"Girls," said Meg seriously, looking from the tumbled head beside her to the two little night-capped ones, "Mother wants us to read and love and mind these books, and we must begin at once. We used to be faithful about it, but since Father went away and all this war trouble unsettled us, we have neglected many things. You can do as you please, but I shall keep my book on the table here and read a little every morning as soon as I wake, for I know it will do me good and help me through the day."

Then she opened her new book and began to read. Jo put her arm round her and, leaning cheek to cheek, read also, with the quiet expression so seldom seen on her restless face.

"How good Meg is! Come, Amy, let's do as they do. I'll help you with the hard words, and they'll explain things if we don't understand," whispered Beth, very much impressed by the pretty books and her sisters' example.

"I'm glad mine is blue," said Amy. And then the rooms were very still while the pages were softly turned, and the winter sunshine crept in to touch the bright heads and serious faces with a Christmas greeting.

Photograph by Jessie Walker

Christmas Eve Homage

Chris Ahlemann

The family walks with eager steps
Through gently falling snow
To where the small brick church awaits,
Its windows all aglow.

They enter then with earnest hearts
And quickly find a pew;
Their spirits stir at organ tones
Of carols old, yet new.

Each listens then in reverent awe
At the story which unfolds,
Of how Love came to earth one night
In a stable rude and cold.

Their heads then bow in silent prayer
While angels hover near,
And grateful hearts give up to God
The present of a tear.

And when at last it's time to go,
They leave with quiet joy;
For tonight their lives were born anew
As they glimpsed God's baby boy.

I do not know a grander effect of music
on the moral feelings than to hear the full
choir and the pealing organ performing a
Christmas anthem in a cathedral.
— Washington Irving

Photograph by William H. Johnson

THROUGH MY WINDOW

Pamela Kennedy

MARY'S JOURNEY

The dust danced in a golden sunbeam as the young girl studied the space just before her. She shook her head slightly. She wondered if she were dreaming. Then, with a rush, the experiences of a few moments ago swirled in her mind: the angel, the announcement, the question, the promise, her agreement. She raised her hand to her face. Somehow the familiar contours of her cheek and jaw reassured her. She was still Mary of Nazareth, betrothed to Joseph the carpenter. Then she caught her breath. She was also something else. She moved her hand to her waist and held it there a moment, hearing the echo of the heavenly messenger, "You shall conceive and bring forth a son, and shall call him Jesus. The Holy Spirit will come upon you and through the power of the Highest, the child you bear will be called the Son of God. Your cousin, Elisabeth, has also conceived a child in her old age. For with God, nothing is impossible."

Elisabeth! Mary gathered her shawl around her head and ran from the room. Gathering a few belongings, she quickly located a group of pilgrims who were traveling south towards Judea. Soon she could be at the hillside home of Zacharias and Elisabeth.

As she walked the dusty Galilean road, the angelic message tumbled in her mind. How could it be true? And yet, how could it not? Hundreds of years earlier had not the prophet Isaiah spoken of a holy child, a Messiah, born of a virgin? Surely, she was not that woman. But the angel told her she had found favor with God, that she was blessed. Impossible. Then she recalled his last few words: "With God, nothing is impossible." She hurried along, anxious to see her cousin.

Leaving the other travelers, Mary climbed the path leading to the home of Zacharias. Bursting in the door she called "Elisabeth! Elisabeth! It's Mary!"

"Child!" the older woman cried. Mary's heart jumped as she saw the bulge of pregnancy under Elisabeth's robes. Then her cousin reached out to her. "Oh, Mary, you are truly blessed as is the child in your womb! How wonderful it is that the mother of my Lord should come to me! The moment I heard your greeting, the babe growing in me leaped for joy!"

Mary could not believe her ears. How could Elisabeth know? Mary was overwhelmed. It was true! Amazingly, impossibly, miraculously true! She laughed out loud and, recalling the words of Hannah from the ancient Scriptures, she burst forth: "My soul magnifies the Lord and my spirit rejoices in God, my Savior. For He that is mighty has done great things for me. Holy is His name."

She fell into the arms of Elisabeth, and the two of them stood there a long time, laughing and weeping for joy.

"Come," Elisabeth said finally, "you must stay with us. My child will not be born for a few more months. There is so much for us to talk about."

Mary's fears subsided in the warm glow of Elisabeth's love. Day after day they walked and talked about God and about the sons they would bear. They marveled at the mysteries of the Lord and how He could use them, two simple women, to accomplish His purposes. As Elisabeth's child grew, so did Mary's faith. How great was God's love!

All too quickly, three months passed. Mary knew she could not remain in Judea much longer. It was nearly time for Elisabeth's baby to be born and time for Mary to step into her own future. The day they parted was one of both sorrow and joy. The older woman gave the younger a bundle of carefully folded swaddling clothes, a gift for the unborn child. They embraced one last time, and then Mary turned and hurried down the hillside.

Mary's fears subsided in the warm glow of Elisabeth's love.

Turning her back on the safety of her relatives' home, she set her face towards Nazareth and the reality that lay before her. What would Joseph think? Would he believe her? What about their betrothal vows? Already she had felt the tiny flutter of new life within her womb. It was no longer just a possibility. She was most certainly with child. When she slept at night, huddled under the dark canopy of the summer sky, her dreams were filled with anxious visions. Angels sang songs of praise to God, but their choruses were interrupted by the angry voices of townspeople calling out her shame. And Joseph, dear Joseph. His face appeared in her dreams as well. He was confused, disappointed, unbelieving.

In the morning she woke, braided her hair, and dusted off her cloak. Silently she prayed as she continued the last few miles into Nazareth. Then, as the town came into view, she felt the warm rays of the rising sun against her back. It felt like God's loving embrace, driving the fear and apprehension from her heart.

Mary raised her chin and set her eyes upon her home, her future. Then, as clearly as she had heard them the first time, the words of Gabriel echoed in her mind once more: "With God, nothing is impossible."

Original artwork by Doris Ettlinger
Photograph by Londie Padelsky

CHRISTMAS! THE VERY
WORD BRINGS
JOY TO OUR HEARTS.
—JOAN WINMILL BROWN

THE ANNUNCIATION

Luke 1: 26–33

—⁓—

And in the sixth month the angel Gabriel was sent from God unto a city of Galilee, named Nazareth, to a virgin espoused to a man whose name was Joseph, of the house of David; and the virgin's name was Mary.

And the angel came in unto her, and said, Hail, thou that art highly favoured, the Lord is with thee: blessed art thou among women.

And when she saw him, she was troubled at his saying, and cast in her mind what manner of salutation this should be.

And the angel said unto her, Fear not, Mary: for thou hast found favour with God.

And, behold, thou shalt conceive in thy womb, and bring forth a son, and shalt call his name JESUS.

He shall be great, and shall be called the Son of the Highest: and the Lord God shall give unto him the throne of his father David:

And he shall reign over the house of Jacob for ever; and of his kingdom there shall be no end.

THE ANNUNCIATION *by John William Waterhouse (1849–1917). Image provided by Fine Art Photographic Library, Ltd., London.*

THE NATIVITY

Luke 2: 1–7

And it came to pass in those days, that there went out a decree from Caesar Augustus, that all the world should be taxed. (And this taxing was first made when Cyrenius was governor of Syria.)

And all went to be taxed, every one into his own city.

And Joseph also went up from Galilee, out of the city of Nazareth, into Judaea, unto the city of David, which is called Bethlehem; (because he was of the house and lineage of David:) to be taxed with Mary his espoused wife, being great with child.

And so it was, that, while they were there, the days were accomplished that she should be delivered.

And she brought forth her firstborn son, and wrapped him in swaddling clothes, and laid him in a manger; because there was no room for them in the inn.

NATIVITY *by Charles Poerson (1609–1667).
Photograph by Gérard Blot. Image provided
by Art Resource NY/Réunion des Musées
Nationaux/Louvre, Paris, France.*

ANGELS AND HEPHERDS

Luke 2: 8–14

And there were in the same country shepherds abiding in the field, keeping watch over their flock by night.

And, lo, the angel of the Lord came upon them, and the glory of the Lord shone round about them: and they were sore afraid.

And the angel said unto them, Fear not: for, behold, I bring you good tidings of great joy, which shall be to all people.

For unto you is born this day in the city of David a Saviour, which is Christ the Lord. And this shall be a sign unto you; Ye shall find the babe wrapped in swaddling clothes, lying in a manger.

And suddenly there was with the angel a multitude of the heavenly host praising God, and saying,

Glory to God in the highest, and on earth peace, good will toward men.

THE ADORATION OF THE SHEPHERDS *by Lorenzo Lotto (1480–1536). Photograph by Eric Lessing. Image provided by Art Resource NY/Musei Civici d'Arte e Storia/Brescia, Italy.*

Adoration
OF
THE MAGI

Matthew 2: 7–12

—⁊⁊⁊—

Then Herod, when he had privily called the wise men, inquired of them diligently what time the star appeared.

And he sent them to Bethlehem, and said, Go and search diligently for the young child; and when ye have found him, bring me word again, that I may come and worship him also.

When they had heard the king, they departed; and, lo, the star, which they saw in the east, went before them, till it came and stood over where the young child was.

When they saw the star, they rejoiced with exceeding great joy.

And when they were come into the house, they saw the young child with Mary his mother, and fell down, and worshipped him: and when they had opened their treasures, they presented unto him gifts; gold, and frankincense, and myrrh.

And being warned of God in a dream that they should not return to Herod, they departed into their own country another way.

ADORATION OF THE MAGI *by Antonio Balestra (1666–1740). Image provided by Cameraphoto/ Art Resource/S. Zaccaria, Venice, Italy.*

THE FLIGHT INTO EGYPT

Matthew 2:13–15

—⁓—

And when they were departed, behold, the angel of the Lord appeareth to Joseph in a dream, saying, Arise, and take the young child and his mother, and flee into Egypt, and be thou there until I bring thee word: for Herod will seek the young child to destroy him.

When he arose, he took the young child and his mother by night, and departed into Egypt:

And was there until the death of Herod: that it might be fulfilled which was spoken of the Lord by the prophet, saying, Out of Egypt have I called my son.

We consider **Christmas** as the
encounter, the great encounter, the
historical encounter, the decisive
encounter, between **God** and
mankind. He who has faith knows
this truly; let him rejoice.

—Pope Paul VI, December 23, 1965

The Most Perfect Gift

Micheline Hull Dolan

No blanket of white
To cover the ground,
No pines brightly glowing
With lights all around,

No presents tied gaily
With ribbon of red,
Just a pillow of straw
For the infant's sweet head.

A mother's sweet song
Broke the silence that night.
A brilliant white star
Turned darkness to light.

The birth in the manger,
Pure love we recall,
God's most perfect Christmas
Gift to us all.

A Christmas Carol

Josiah Gilbert Holland

There's a song in the air!
　　There's a star in the sky!
　　There's a mother's deep prayer
　　And a baby's low cry!
And the star rains its fire while the Beautiful sing,
For the manger of Bethlehem cradles a king.

　　There's a tumult of joy
　　O'er the wonderful birth,
　　For the virgin's sweet boy
　　Is the Lord of the earth.
Ay! the star rains its fire and the Beautiful sing,
For the manger of Bethlehem cradles a king.

　　In the light of that star
　　Lie the ages impearled;
　　And that song from afar
　　Has swept over the world.
Every hearth is aflame, and the Beautiful sing
In the homes of the nations that Jesus is King.

　　We rejoice in the light,
　　And we echo the song
　　That comes down through the night
　　From the heavenly throng.
Ay! we shout to the lovely evangel they bring,
And we greet in his cradle our Savior and King.

Photograph by William H. Johnson

Weathervanes FOR Steeples

Ralph W. Seager

In Guyanoga valley we located a farmer by his big, red barn; it was his landmark, his identity and signature. His house showed up later. Folks would answer queries by saying, "Yep, that's White's barn up there on East Hill," or, "Cole's is the first barn up Belknap Hill." A stranger might wonder whether he would find a house at all, and he would have to wonder until he got there. The first thing to know about a Guyanoga farmer was where his barn sat. Everything else came in second.

His silo was nearly as significant, standing like a lighthouse far from sea, yet raised in that white imagery. When the sun got tired and dropped its head on the shoulders of evening, these silos would catch the last rays upon their domes, light up, and become beacons across the western side of day. It was then that the farmers would turn their plows at dusk and head for home.

Many a Guyanoga boy first learned the meaning of holy and sacred not in church, but within his father's barn. He came face-on with Christmas the night the baby lamb was born. When Old Dobbin was down in his stall and could not get up, he came to grips with his own Gethsemane. Before he could spell the word or know its meaning, he was down on his blue-patched knees asking for it not to happen. Easter came first— handed to him when his new calf stood up on knobby stilts all wet and shining and trembling, and the boy trembled too, seeing that life was getting better than ever.

This was his first church. Here he became acquainted with birth and life and death, with the peace of animals upon it all. He learned about barns and granaries and bushels, sheep and horses, the cattle on a thousand hills, doves on the rafters, the mice under the threshing floor; for none of these creatures had given up on the Bible. They were still in it as they have been for thousands of years. They always will be.

> THE FIRST AND BEST BARN WE KNOW CRADLED THE LIGHT OF THE WORLD.

The first and best barn we know cradled the Light of the World. Yet, across the print of literature, the hounds of prejudice and bigotry have always snapped at the innkeeper. Here was a man who knew that whatever else Mary

Photograph by Dennis Frates

needed in that wide night, she needed peace. And there was peace in the stable: the peace of cudding cows, of gentle ewes. Farmers of every age know that this man gave the best he had, his barn, better by far than the inn. For the stable offered serenity against turmoil, sharing against greed, and fellowship against selfishness.

At the inn was confusion amid the stifling press of humanity. There was contention for rooms and most assuredly the flaring of tempers of ill-tempered men. For no one, at any time, is happy on his way to pay taxes. So the innkeeper has lived under the condemnation of most of his fellowmen because he alone had the sense to lead Mary and Joseph to the peace of his mangers, into the warm fragrance of summer, the soft lowing of his cattle, and the white softness of sheep. Where would one find a better beginning for the Good Shepherd? Make no mistake about it, the world owes a debt to the keeper of the inn.

From that time to this, farmers have walked backwards through Christmas. They have reversed the original and have brought the bleating life of their barns into their kitchens. Down through the ages it has fallen to the farmer, he of the countryside, to act out Christmas over and over again. Every time he wraps the new-born lamb in his sweater, bedding it down in the wood-box behind the stove, he has renewed Christmas.

The Christmas Star

Charles A. Heath

Upon a still and starry night
Whose very stillness thrilled
The watch of centuries—the night
When hope would be fulfilled—
Through silent skies
A starlight flies
That God Eternal willed.

While eager eyes first caught its ray
To ages long denied—
Unlike the night, unlike the day,
But glory glorified—
Through singing skies
Hope verifies
That earth is now its sway.

Around heaven high the chorus rang,
Until earth, too, was filled,
For men joined angels as they sang—
So much their hearts were thrilled—
'Neath star-bright skies
The harmonies
No centuries have stilled.

The Holy Star

William Cullen Bryant

As shadows cast by cloud and sun
Flit o'er the summer grass,
So, in Thy sight, Almighty One,
Earth's generations pass.

And while the years, an
    endless host,
Come pressing swiftly on,
The brightest names that
    earth can boast
Just glisten and are gone.

Yet doth the Star of
    Bethlehem shed
A luster pure and sweet,
And still it leads, as once it led,
To the Messiah's feet.

O Father, may that holy star
Grow every year more bright,
And send its glorious beams afar
To fill the world with light.

Photograph by Nancy Matthews

Beneath the Winter Stars

Grace Noll Crowell

How white the stars are in this inky blackness!
How strangely still the hills and hollows lie!
How cold beneath the passionless white fires
That burn like molten silver in the sky!
I am so small beneath their countless numbers,
So little and so lost in this vast dark;
I reach my hands to find some warmth and comfort
In fires a million light years off, each spark
Left smoldering from the white heat of creation:
Strange, icy flames that have the power to sear
Upon my heart how truly unimportant
Is this small earth and man's brief sojourn here. . . .
And yet, and yet, recalling God's great mercy
In sending Christ to tread this planet's sod,
I straighten in the starlight; I grow taller,
Remembering my significance to God.

I, SHORTER-LIVED THAN ANY TREE,

CAN STAND AND FEEL ETERNITY

WHEEL ABOUT ME IN THE FAR,

LONELY ORBIT OF A STAR.

—ROBERT P. TRISTRAM COFFIN

Photograph by Christopher Talbot Frank

THE NEW YEAR

Gladys Taber

What the new year will bring, we cannot know. I think of the year that has been folded away in time. There has been much good in it, although some sorrow; but there are always, in any year, many lovely memories, and I shall cherish them. Life is not, for most of us, a pageant of splendor but is made up of many small things, rather like an old-fashioned piecework quilt. No two people have the same, but we all have our own, whether it be listening to Beethoven's Fifth with a beloved friend or seeing a neighbor at the back door with a basket of white dahlias. Or after a long, hard day having the family say, "That was a good supper."

As the clock moves irrevocably from yesterday to today, I go out on the terrace and fill my heart with the intensity of the winter moonlight. This is the time when the heart is at peace and the spirit rests. I think of the words, "Be still, and know that I am God." Far off a branch falls in the old orchard, and sometimes a plane goes overhead bound for a far destination. I wish the pilot well, in that cold sky, and hope the passengers come safely home. Silently I say, "Happy New Year to all of us, all over this turning earth. And may we make it a year of loving-kindness and gentle hearts."

Photograph by Larry LeFever/Grant Heilman

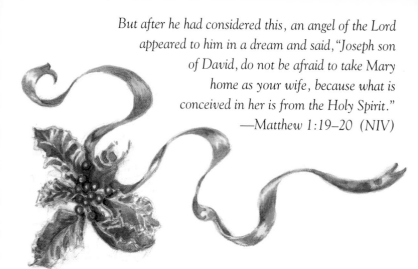

But after he had considered this, an angel of the Lord appeared to him in a dream and said, "Joseph son of David, do not be afraid to take Mary home as your wife, because what is conceived in her is from the Holy Spirit."
—Matthew 1:19–20 (NIV)

DEVOTIONS FROM THE HEART

Pamela Kennedy

GOD HAS A BETTER IDEA

I have often thought that Joseph is a somewhat overlooked participant of the Christmas story. There he was, minding his own business in the carpenter shop, contemplating his engagement, when suddenly his fiancée, Mary, takes off for a three-month visit to her cousin, Elisabeth; and when Mary returns, she announces she is expecting. This would be shocking enough news to report in our day and age; but back in the first century, it could have been been grounds for a death sentence!

Joseph faces a very serious dilemma. According to the customs and practices of his time, he has two options: He could divorce Mary quietly for breaking their engagement vows, which are as binding as marriage vows, or he could denounce her publicly and hand her over to the religious leaders, who have the legal authority to call for her death by stoning. His decision places him both at the sidelines and at the center of a huge drama. He had to have wondered, who is the father of Mary's baby? What has Mary done? What should he do?

We know from Matthew's account that Joseph was a man who considered things carefully. He was not impulsive, nor was he arrogant. After weighing his options, Joseph decides he will divorce Mary quietly. Although people might assume that he was weak, or worse, complicit in this apparent moral indiscretion, Joseph is unwilling to see Mary punished or publicly disgraced. Joseph's primary concern is not for himself; it is for the woman he loves. Joseph's decision exposes his character and leaves room for God's compassion.

In the dark night of Joseph's contemplation, God sends an angel who presents Joseph with a third option. For Joseph to accept this angelic revelation requires both faith and courage. He must believe the word of God and step away from the dictates of his culture. And Joseph again proves himself a man of integrity. He agrees that God

has a better plan for him; and, in faith, he steps out to take Mary's hand in marriage. Together, they walk into their future.

How often do we ourselves struggle with decisions that seem difficult and overwhelming? We cast about in our minds for solutions, weighing one option against another, trying to determine the best course of action. What should we do when faced with difficult dilemmas? Should we assert what we

---

Dear Father, this Advent season let me set aside my own ideas long enough to ask what You would have me do. Then give me the courage and humility I need to follow the path You set before me. Amen.

---

believe to be our rights or choose to submit to the will of another? Should we demand justice or extend mercy? What if we considered the way of Joseph and opened our hearts to the possibility that God might have another, better idea? What if we set aside our own agendas and prayerfully waited, in the dark night of our uncertainty, for the Lord to reveal his plan?

Could it be that in our searching we would discover, just as Joseph does, that God has a better plan for us?

This Christmas, revel in the triumphant song of the angels and the expectant awe of the shepherds. Wonder at the impossible miracle worked by God in the life of a young Galilean girl. Journey with the Magi along the path of wisdom in search of a King and Savior. And remember to appreciate the gentle courage of Joseph, who set aside his own decisions in order to embrace the plans of God. Be brave enough to admit, in the midst of your personal quandaries, that God just might have a better idea.

Photograph by Dennis Frates